Check out all of the books in the Tell Me About Dinosaurs Series

Published in the United States by Xist Publishing
www.xistpublishing.com
© 2025 Copyright Xist Publishing

First Edition
Hardcover ISBN: 978-1-5324-5495-0
Paperback ISBN: 978-1-5324-5496-7
eISBN: 978-1-5324-5494-3

PUBLISHED IN TEXAS

Tell Me About Dinosaurs
SPINOSAURUS

Marjorie Seevers

xist Publishing

3

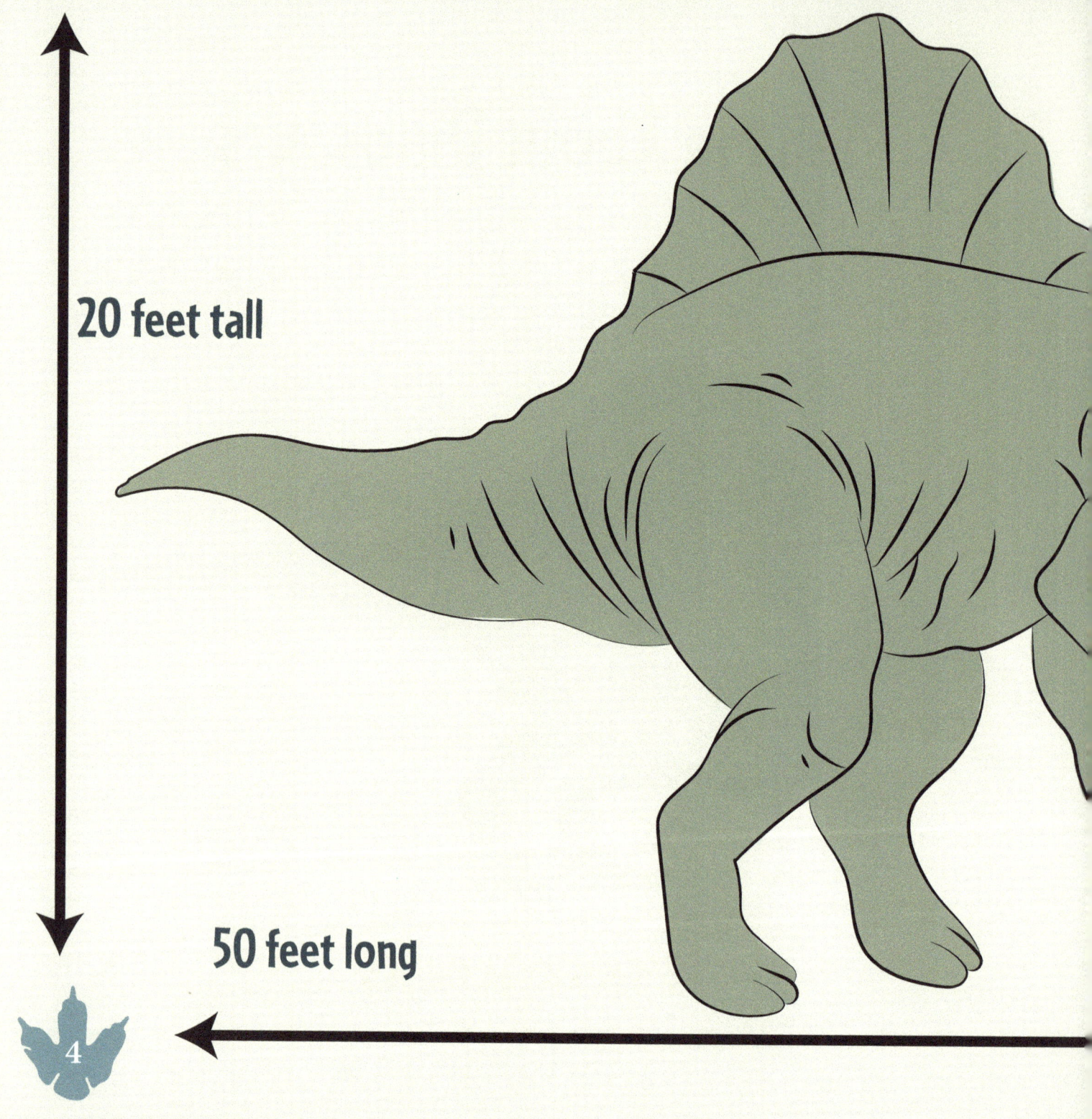

20 feet tall

50 feet long

4

Spinosaurus was a very big dinosaur.

It ate fish and meat.

Spinosaurus had a long, narrow snout.

It had a sail on its back.

Spinosaurus could swim.

It had lots of sharp teeth.

Spinosaurus bones
are called fossils.

Which dinosaur is a Spinosaurus?

What did Spinosaurus eat?